in the news™

BAILOUT! Government Intervention in Business

Bethany Bezdecheck

ROSEN
PUBLISHING®

New York

For Maximus

Published in 2011 by The Rosen Publishing Group, Inc.
29 East 21st Street, New York, NY 10010

Copyright © 2011 by The Rosen Publishing Group, Inc.

First Edition

Library of Congress Cataloging-in-Publication Data

Bezdecheck, Bethany.
Bailout! : government intervention in business / Bethany Bezdecheck. — 1st ed.
       p. cm. — (In the news)
Includes bibliographical references and index.
ISBN 978-1-4358-9449-5 (library binding) —
ISBN 978-1-4488-1681-1 (pbk.) —
ISBN 978-1-4488-1689-7 (6-pack)
1. Bankruptcy—Government policy—United States—Juvenile literature.
2. Industrial policy—United States—Juvenile literature. 3.
Corporations—United States—Finance—Juvenile literature. I. Title.
HG3766.B49 2010
338.6—dc22

2009052247

Manufactured in the United States of America

CPSIA Compliance Information: Batch #S10YA: For further information, contact Rosen Publishing, New York, New York, at 1-800-237-9932.

On the cover: Top left: Many luxury automobile manufacturers were forced to sell cars at lower prices as the economy dipped. Top right: The American International Group (AIG) received a bailout in 2008. Bottom: Protestors question the controversial bailouts.

contents

Corporate Bailouts Explained

In 2008, the United States officially entered into a deep recession, which is a slowdown of economic activity over an extended period of time. Many big businesses were closing, the public was spending far less money than usual, and the national debt was growing at a rapid pace. With fewer products being purchased, many companies could no longer afford to pay their employees. People began to lose their jobs, and in just one year, the nation's unemployment rate had risen by nearly 50 percent. Many argued that not since the Great Depression in the 1930s had the American economy performed so poorly.

During this period of major economic crisis, the public looked anxiously to the federal government for a solution. They wanted to know, "How will things be resolved?" The government's response was that the economy would be restored through the help of corporate bailouts. This answer was very confusing to most

In 2008, the recession led many people to file for unemployment. Once a person files for unemployment, he or she may temporarily receive money from the government while searching for a new job.

people. The majority of U.S. residents weren't quite sure what corporate bailouts were or how they were supposed to help the economy and themselves.

A corporate bailout occurs when the government gives money to a company on the verge of bankruptcy. In most cases, the U.S. government leaves bankrupt companies to fend for themselves. After all, if the government were to give money to every company in danger of going bankrupt, it would have no money left for services like building schools, repairing roads, or providing medical services to the elderly. In addition, one of the principles of the U.S. government is that it should interfere as little as possible in private business dealings. However, some companies are so big that if they were to go bankrupt, they would hurt more than just themselves—they would hurt the entire country.

Stocks and Bonds

In order to understand how big business bankruptcy can affect all of America, it is important to understand corporations and the selling of stocks and bonds. Corporations are companies that make money not only by selling goods and services, but also by selling stocks and bonds. Such companies are referred to as "publicly traded." When a person buys stock in a company, he or she is buying the opportunity to make more money if the company does well. The better a company does, the higher its stock price rises. When stock prices rise, stockholders are able to sell their stock to somebody else for a price greater than what they originally paid for it. The extra money they make through this sale is called a profit.

Unfortunately, stockholders don't always make a profit. When a corporation starts to lose money, its stock price drops. When this happens, many stockholders choose to hold on to their stock, rather than rush to sell it. Instead, they hope that business will pick up again and that they will still be able to one day make a profit. If the company continues to do poorly, however, stockholders may decide they have no choice but to sell their stock. Sometimes they have to sell at a price that is much lower than the price they originally paid. In these cases, the stockholders are losing money, rather than making a profit.

The public can also invest in corporations by buying bonds. Bonds are like loans—the corporation promises to pay back the buyers of bonds while also paying them an additional fee, called interest. The amount of interest paid to the buyer depends on the bond's value at

At the New York Stock Exchange, traders buy and sell stock on behalf of investors. The stock exchange floor resembles a noisy auction as traders work frantically to get their clients the best deals possible.

the time of sale. If the corporation is doing well, the interest rate will generally be higher, as will the initial price of the bond itself. If the corporation is not doing so well, the bond will be less expensive to buy, but the interest paid to the buyer will be lower.

Big businesses like Microsoft, Boeing, and Ford have many investors. People invest money in these businesses because they trust them to do well. They know these businesses have been around a long time, and that they have seen a lot of success. However, history has proven that even the biggest, most powerful corporations can go bankrupt.

The Top Ten Companies of 2009

The Fortune 500 is a list of companies compiled by *Fortune* magazine. The companies are ranked according to their gross revenue and the total amount of income they receive. The following companies were at the top of the Fortune 500 list in 2009:

1. Exxon Mobil
2. Walmart
3. Chevron
4. ConocoPhillips
5. General Electric
6. General Motors
7. Ford
8. AT&T
9. Hewlett-Packard
10. Valero Energy

Reasons for Bankruptcy

There are many reasons why a corporation might face bankruptcy. Sometimes the demand for a company's product decreases. For example, when flat-screen televisions were invented, companies selling only cathode-ray tube (CRT) television sets lost business because more and more people preferred the flat-screen variety. Businesses that lose investors' trust are in danger of going bankrupt as well. If a business commits fraud—

When the flat-screen TV was invented, companies selling only CRT sets knew they would lose business if they did not start investing in flat-screen technology.

uses money in an illegal manner—fewer people will want to buy stocks and bonds from that company.

When a big business goes bankrupt, it can affect the entire economy. Not only do thousands of employees lose their jobs when a large corporation goes bankrupt, but many stockholders who once trusted the corporation with their money also lose their often very large investments. The unemployment rate rises, and people find they have less money to spend. They hold on to their cash just in case things get even worse. With less money being spent on goods and services, even more corporations begin to suffer. This can cause the economy to go into a downward spiral with negative effects that are felt by everyone.

There are corporations in America that are so big and have so many investors that if they do go bankrupt, they have the potential to cause many other businesses to fail. Businesses in danger of having such a negative affect on the economy are known as being too big to fail, or TBTF. The federal government has vowed that if TBTF businesses start to crash, it will seriously consider bailing them out, or providing them with money, in order to protect the rest of the economy.

In 1913, the government created the Federal Reserve, a central banking system designed to give money to TBTF businesses facing bankruptcy. The Federal Reserve continues to exist today, and the money contained within it is supplied by U.S. taxpayers. This means that when big businesses are doing poorly, taxes may be raised in order to increase the money available in the Federal Reserve. However, corporate bailouts do not always result in a healthier economy. Just because a corporation is given some extra money doesn't necessarily mean it will be able to get back on its feet. The public may continue to distrust the corporation, meaning that fewer people will be willing to buy their goods, services, stocks, and bonds. It may also be that after laying off so many employees, the company is understaffed and has trouble operating at full capacity. Reasons like these make tax increases for the purpose of assisting failing corporations controversial.

Corporate Bailout Controversy

There are two sides to the argument about corporate bailouts. Some people are for them. Some are against.

People who agree with corporate bailouts may feel that while no one likes paying more taxes, it is sometimes necessary to do so in order to keep the economy up and running. They remind their opponents that if certain corporations go bankrupt, the entire population may be at risk of losing money. They tend to argue that while

Many Americans have openly protested corporate bailouts. The protestors pictured here believe that corporate executives who have mismanaged funds should go to jail instead of receive government money.

not all corporate bailouts are successful, the government will never know whether or not a corporation can be saved through a bailout unless it gives it a try.

Those who oppose bailouts may argue that taxpayers should not have to pay for mistakes made by big corporations. They might feel it doesn't make sense to try and help the economy by raising the taxes of people who are already lacking money. They may also feel that it isn't fair for big businesses to receive government support while small companies and individuals continue to struggle daily. Finally, people who are against corporate bailouts argue that businesses that are too big to fail may engage in bad business practices because they know that no matter what they do, there is a good chance that the government will come to their rescue.

Despite the well-known controversy surrounding corporate bailouts, the government continues to stand by its decision to use the Federal Reserve to help TBTF companies.

Prerecession Bailouts

It wasn't until the 2008 recession that corporate bailouts became a hot topic. But in reality, the U.S. government had already been bailing out corporations for many years. After all, it doesn't always take a recession for big businesses to go bankrupt. Some of the most interesting corporate bailouts occurred before the year 2000.

The Penn Central Transportation Company

In 1956, President Dwight D. Eisenhower signed the Federal Aid Highway Act, which created 41,000 miles (65,983 kilometers) of new interstate highways. In the Northeast, many people had been taking the train to other states for work. However, the new highways meant that these people could now drive their cars to work instead. With more people driving and fewer people buying train tickets, the railroads in the Northeast began to lose a lot of business.

It was President Eisenhower's hope that the Federal Aid Highway Act would make it easier for Americans to commute to other states for work.

In 1968, the Pennsylvania Railroad, the New York City Railroad, and the New Haven and Hartford Railroad decided they would save their companies by combining forces. They formed a new corporation called the Penn Central Transportation Company. They figured that by becoming one big corporation, they would become a stronger, more powerful force, and business would pick up for them again.

The combining of two or more companies is known as either a merger or an acquisition. In the case of a merger, companies enter into a voluntary agreement to join forces. When the two or more companies become one, responsibilities and income are shared equally. In an acquisition, a stronger company acquires, or buys, a weaker company. The stronger company takes control of the weaker company's assets but must also take responsibility for the weaker company's debts.

Unfortunately, the Penn Central Transportation Company merger was not a success. The three railroads had a difficult time agreeing on how to do business. They spent more time arguing among themselves than they did on trying to convince people to take the train instead of driving. Before long, the new Penn Central Transportation Company found itself on the verge of bankruptcy.

Although railroads were no longer a very popular form of transportation, many people had invested money in the creation of Penn Central. The idea of three historic corporations coming together to form one new corporation excited people so much that they forgot about the decrease in the demand for railroads. By the time Penn Central was doomed to fail, many investors were doomed to fail along with it.

The government knew that with so many investors committed to Penn Central, the closing of the corporation would be devastating to the American economy. In 1970, it bailed out Penn Central by giving it nearly $700 million to grant to its creditors. While this money meant that the railroad's investors would not be hurt financially, the bailout wasn't enough to keep Penn Central going. In 1976, the government chose to merge the corporation with five other struggling railroads. The new business was named the Consolidated Rail Corporation, otherwise known as Conrail.

Although it continued to receive billions of dollars in government aid, Conrail was not a success at first. However, two different government acts enabled the company to eventually make a profit. The first was the Staggers Act of 1980, which loosened the government's control on the rates that railroads were allowed to charge. The second was the Northeast Rail Service Act of 1981, which made Conrail exempt from paying state taxes.

The Penn Central bailout was a costly, complicated series of events that didn't go as smoothly as the government probably hoped for. In the end, however, the bailout did prevent the economy from taking a mighty tumble. The next big corporate bailout would prove to be a much bigger triumph.

Lockheed and Rolls-Royce

In 1971, the federal government created the Emergency Loan Guarantee Act, which gave the government the power to lend funds to any big business facing bank-

Turbofans manufactured by Lockheed and Rolls-Royce were designed to save customers money by burning less fuel, but they would prove to be too expensive to make.

ruptcy. The first recipient of a bailout under this act was aerospace giant Lockheed. Around the time of the Penn Central crisis, Lockheed was working on building a new large airliner called the TriStar. In order to build the three-engine TriStar, Lockheed partnered with another corporation, Rolls-Royce. Besides cars, Rolls–Royce also builds a variety of engines for many industries, among them the aerospace and aviation industry.

Rolls-Royce planned to make the TriStar jet engines burn less fuel by using a new technology, called turbofans. Unfortunately, the turbofans were so expensive to produce that Rolls-Royce was driven to bankruptcy before the TriStar jets could take flight. Because Lockheed couldn't sell jets without jet engines, the corporation was unable to make back the money it had invested in creating the TriStar. In 1971, the same year that the Emergency Loan Guarantee Act was passed, Lockheed turned to the government for support.

Because Lockheed built aircraft, spacecraft, and other equipment for the U.S. military, the government felt it was especially important for it to survive. One could even say that the safety of the entire country and its assets abroad were at stake. Bailing out Lockheed also meant that thousands of Californians working for the corporation would be able to keep their jobs. Happily, the bailout was a success. By 1977, Lockheed had paid off its government loans, and the government had earned millions of dollars in interest fees. Not only that, but the TriStar was eventually completed and went on to become one of the most celebrated passenger aircrafts of its time.

Other Significant Bailouts

During the next ten years, the government bailed out three more corporations. The first was the Franklin National Bank, which collapsed in 1974 due to corruption. Italian financier Michele Sindona—who is suspected to have had links to the Sicilian Mafia—purchased control-

Michele Sindona is just one of many business-people who have used their influence over the corporate market to illegally increase their personal wealth.

ling interest in the bank from Laurence Tisch, chairman of Loews Corporation. Tisch was later sued for accepting a large amount of money for the stock while knowing all along that Sindona intended to use his power of investment to break the law. Sindona became vice chairman of the bank and used his new role to transfer funds and issue credit to the Italian drug market. His scheming did not go on forever, however. He was eventually convicted of fraud, and the Franklin National Bank went bankrupt as a result. The federal government bailed out Franklin National and sold it to European American Bank. Sindona died in prison due to poisoning. While some say he was murdered, others claim he committed suicide.

The Chrysler Corporation's trouble began when consumers became more interested in Japanese cars. These were generally cheaper and used less gas than American automobiles. This resulted in a loss of business for Chrysler, which greatly troubled the government. Worried that Chrysler's bankruptcy would bring down the entire automotive industry, the government created the Chrysler Loan Guarantee Act of 1980. The act gave the government the power to loan Chrysler $1.5 billion in aid.

The third corporation receiving a government bailout was the Continental Illinois National Bank and Trust, which was once the seventh-largest bank in the country. This bank became unstable after lending money to big oil companies during a time when the oil industry was doing poorly. When the oil companies were unable to pay loan fees to the Continental Illinois National Bank and Trust, large depositors panicked and withdrew $10 billion in deposits in 1984. When it became clear that the bank was sure to fail, the government provided it with $4.5 billion in emergency funds.

In the late 1980s, 745 savings and loan associations were in a state of financial crisis. Savings and loan associations are companies that accept savings deposits, as well as loan people money for buying homes. During the 1970s, the housing market experienced a boom. Many people were looking to buy new homes. This boom excited the savings and loan associations. They

When President George H. W. Bush signed the Financial Institutions Reform, Recovery, and Enforcement Act, he may not have foreseen that giving government-sponsored enterprises more control over the housing market would help contribute to a recession.

were eager to experience an increase in customers. They began to lend more and more people money, thinking they would make a huge profit once their many new customers paid them interest fees. However, in 1986, the housing market slowed down unexpectedly. This caused the savings and loan associations to regret lending such a large amount of money to their customers. If they had been more careful, they would have been able to handle the sudden drop in business. Instead, they now had so little money that all 745 of them were now on the brink of bankruptcy.

The government was extremely worried about the savings and loan situation. If 745 big businesses went bankrupt, the American economy would be in serious trouble. In 1989, President George H. W. Bush signed the Financial Institutions Reform, Recovery, and Enforcement Act. The act not only bailed out the savings and loan associations, but it also created a new set of rules and regulations for them to follow. It was the government's hope that these new rules and regulations would prevent the associations from loaning too much money ever again. Of course, bailing out so many companies was very costly. The Financial Institutions Reform, Recovery, and Enforcement Act gave the savings and loan institutions nearly $300 billion, the majority of which was provided by taxpayers. This decision was not popular among the public—no one likes having to pay more taxes.

The Financial Institutions Reform, Recovery, and Enforcement Act's Rules and Regulations

1. The Office of Thrift Supervision would monitor, examine, and supervise savings institutions.
2. The Federal Housing Finance Board would oversee federal home loan banks.
3. The results of the savings and loan associations' performance evaluation would be made available to the public.

4. Mortgage lenders would be required to collect and report data on mortgage activities.

5. The Appraisal Subcommittee would ensure that new regulations for real estate appraisals would be met.

6. Government-sponsored enterprises Fannie Mae and Freddie Mac would be given additional responsibilities in supporting mortgages for low-income families.

Bailouts in the Current Recession

Fortunately, the government did not have to bail out a corporation for another twelve years. This gave the economy some time to recover. It also gave taxpayers some time to calm down about having to pay for the savings and loan associations' mistake. Business began to boom once more, and the next bailout would not be the result of bad corporate decisions. Instead, it would be the result of fear.

On September 11, 2001, the United States was attacked by terrorists from the Islamic group Al Qaeda. Taught to believe that the United States was an evil power, nineteen Al Qaeda members hijacked passenger planes and flew them into the World Trade Center towers in New York City, as well as into the Pentagon in Washington, D.C. Another plane that was allegedly on its way to the White House crashed before reaching its des-

Grounding airlines after 9/11 left many airplane passengers stranded. With no way of returning home, they were trapped in out-of-commission airports far away from their friends and family.

tination. The attacks resulted in the deaths of nearly three thousand people.

Immediately after the attacks, the government decided to temporarily shut down all airlines. In fact, all aircraft were banned from flying over the United States unless they belonged to the U.S. government or were on extremely important missions, such as ferrying hospital patients in critical condition. Government officials were nervous about similar attacks occurring and wanted to conduct a thorough investigation before people were allowed to fly again. Being grounded caused the airlines to lose a great deal of money. Once they were back in the air, business was terribly slow. One reason for this was that Americans were afraid to fly. This fear, combined with days of being unable to operate, caused the airline industry to collapse.

President George W. Bush helped the airlines by signing the Air Transportation Safety and System Stabilization Act. The act paid the airlines for the days they had been forced to close. Although the September 11, 2001, attacks were a devastating historical event, the airline bailout was still hundreds of billions of dollars cheaper than the savings and loan bailout in 1989.

Although there were several sizable corporate bailouts during the twentieth century, none of them received nearly as much attention as the bailouts that occurred during the recession of the early 2000s. Because this recession affected such a large percentage of the American public, "corporate bailouts" became a household term about which everyone was buzzing.

The Subprime Mortgage Crisis

Many different situations contributed to the recession of the early 2000s. Two examples include a huge increase in oil prices and a large amount of money being spent on the war in Iraq. Still, most experts agree that the subprime mortgage crisis was the biggest player in the most serious economic slowdown since the Great Depression.

The subprime mortgage crisis got its name from subprime mortgages, which are home loan agreements that made it easier for people with low income and poor credit to purchase homes. Before subprime mortgages existed, qualifying for a mortgage wasn't easy. Mortgage brokers worked to make sure that applicants had good credit, steady jobs, and enough money in the bank to pay their loan fees before approving them for mortgages. Subprime mortgages, however, came with fewer restrictions. Almost anyone who applied for a subprime mortgage was granted approval.

Businesses hoped that subprime mortgages would encourage more people to purchase homes, thereby helping the housing market and boosting the economy. However, because recipients of subprime mortgages had poor credit and less money to spend, it was likely that many of them would be unable to meet their mortgage payments.

What Are Mortgages, and How Do They Work?

When a person wants to buy a home, he or she must apply for a mortgage. A mortgage is a loan agreement

Wells Fargo's Home Mortgage Branch helps people pay for houses. Its other lines of business include commercial banking and consumer finance.

between a borrower—a person looking to buy a home—
and the owner of the mortgage, usually a bank.
Borrowers apply for mortgages through mortgage brokers who work on commission, meaning the amount
of money they make depends on the amount of mortgages they issue. Once a person is approved for a
mortgage by a mortgage broker, he or she pays for the
new home by making loan payments to the bank. Loan
payments are made until the total price of the home
has been paid for, plus interest. If a person is unable
to make his or her mortgage payments, that person
will enter into foreclosure. This means that his or her
lender will take possession of the home and sell it to a
third party in order to raise the money needed to pay
the mortgage.

A Shift in the Housing Market

The fact that borrowers of subprime mortgages were
likely to default on their loan payments did not worry
mortgage brokers. Collecting mortgage payments was
not their responsibility. Once they approved a borrower
for a mortgage, they sold the mortgage to a bank.
Holding on to subprime mortgages made banks nervous,
however. They knew that if borrowers did not pay their
housing bills, the bank would not make back the cost of
the mortgage. Banks therefore sold subprime mortgages

to investment firms, which packaged the mortgages together and sold shares of them to investors.

At first, the subprime mortgage market seemed to be working in everyone's favor. People who were once unqualified for mortgages were now able to buy their own homes. By selling subprime mortgages to investment firms, banks made back the cost of the mortgages without having to collect loan payments. By purchasing the subprime mortgages, investment firms had more shares to sell and were therefore making more money. Still, dealing in subprime mortgages was undoubtedly a risky business, and things just couldn't stay sunny for long.

Between 2006 and 2007, the price of houses dropped unexpectedly. With the housing market making less money than usual, lenders were forced to raise home interest rates in order to make ends meet. Doing this made it even more difficult for subprime mortgage borrowers to pay their bills. More and more people began to default on their loans, causing the value of subprime mortgage shares to decrease. As investors became aware of this problem, they began to change their minds about putting their money toward subprime mortgages. Investment firms started losing a great deal of business. Before long, many of them were headed toward bankruptcy.

Bear Stearns

The first investment firm to fail due to subprime mortgage lending was Bear Stearns, a leading global investment bank founded in 1923. Named the "most admired" investment firm by *Fortune* magazine in 2005, Bear Stearns was not a company that was expected to collapse. However, by the summer of 2007, two of the

Bear Stearns' failure caused many Americans to begin questioning corporate bailouts. Some taxpayers protested that their money should not go toward helping what they felt was a dishonest company.

firm's subprime hedge funds, pools of money made up of subprime mortgages, had lost nearly all of their value.

Bear Stearns' investors were angry. They claimed the firm had not warned them of the risk they were taking in investing in subprime mortgages. A lawsuit was filed against the firm, and when the public learned of this lawsuit, even more people lost faith in the company. Unable to attract new clients, the firm had no choice but to inform the government that it was in need of a corporate bailout.

In March 2008, the Federal Reserve provided Bear Stearns with an emergency loan. Although the loan helped to repay Bear Stearns' investors, it did not help restore people's confidence in the corporation. Bear Stearns continued to have trouble gaining clients. It was apparent that the firm would not survive on its own. Shortly after receiving its federal loan, Bear Stearns was bought by rival financial firm JPMorgan Chase for less than 10 percent of its market value. Because JPMorgan Chase was taking ownership of Bear Stearns' liabilities as well as its assets, the Federal Reserve loaned the firm $30 million to help it deal with Bear Stearns' debts.

Fannie Mae, Freddie Mac, and Lehman Brothers

During this time, the housing market was receiving money from two government-sponsored enterprises.

These enterprises were the Federal National Mortgage Association, otherwise known as Fannie Mae, and the Federal Home Loan Mortgage Corporation, otherwise known as Freddie Mac. The pair was created in order to ensure that mortgage lenders would have enough money to keep the housing market afloat. As government-sponsored enterprises, Fannie Mae and Freddie Mac received financial credit from the government but were still privately owned,

In 2008, the U.S. Treasury Department provided mortgage finance giants Fannie Mae and Freddie Mac with $34.2 billion and $51.7 billion, respectively. By 2010, taxpayers had spent $111 billion bailing out both agencies.

publicly traded corporations. Like investment firms, they bought mortgages from savings and loan organizations and resold them to investors. However, a portion of the profit made through these sales was given to mortgage lenders so that more mortgages could be issued. Money given to lenders by Fannie and Freddie also helped keep lenders out of trouble should their mortgages go unpaid.

Although Fannie and Freddie existed to protect the economy, when the subprime mortgage crisis hit, not even they could save the day. Accounting problems and mismanagement had left them in no condition to give lenders the amount of money needed to effectively help the housing market. In addition, because the public was now so unenthusiastic about investing money in real estate, fewer people were buying Fannie and Freddie's stock. Things looked bleak for the formerly dynamic duo.

The federal government knew that without Fannie and Freddie, the housing market would surely go under. In July 2008, Congress passed the Housing and Economic Recovery Act, thereby creating the Federal Housing Finance Agency (FHFA). The FHFA became Fannie and Freddie's conservator, meaning it would run the two organizations until they were able to get back on their feet.

The FHFA did not take its new role lightly. It swiftly laid down a set of strict rules created to prevent Fannie and Freddie from making further mistakes. It also took control of the pair's assets, assumed power over their officers and directors, suspended stockholders' voting rights, and halted the selling of shares. Of course, simply teaching Fannie and Freddie a lesson wasn't going to fix the economy. Fannie and Freddie needed money—lots of it—if they were to continue to hold up the housing market.

It would take time before Fannie and Freddie were able to help put a stop to the subprime mortgage mess. They certainly couldn't save the additional investment firms that were suffering due to subprime lending.

One such firm was the financial services giant Lehman Brothers. The firm had previously bought a significant number of subprime mortgages. It was now unable to sell enough shares of these risky securities to stay in business. During the first six months of 2008, Lehman Brothers' employees watched in horror as the value of their stock dropped by 73 percent. In August, the firm decided it could no longer afford to keep all of its employees. They announced that fifteen hundred workers would be laid off. Finally, on September 15, Lehman Brothers filed for bankruptcy, marking the largest bankruptcy filing in U.S. history.

The federal government provided Lehman Brothers with financial assistance in exchange for shares in its lower-quality stock. However, like Bear Stearns, Lehman Brothers was so crippled by this time that it could not go back to the way things were. Portions of the company, which had offices around the globe, were sold to Barclays, a British financial services firm, and Nomura Holdings, a Japanese financial holding company.

American International Group (AIG)

A week after the government bailed out Fannie and Freddie, it found itself bailing out the American International Group (AIG), an insurance company with headquarters in New York, London, Paris, and Hong Kong. In 1987, AIG created the AIG Financial Products Corporation, a company that engaged in a variety of financial transactions with customers around the world. In 2007, the company decided to sell subprime mortgages in the form of credit default swaps. A credit default swap is an agreement whereby for an additional fee an investor is guaranteed not to lose money if the debt in which he or she is investing goes unpaid. In other words, if a person defaults on a mortgage, the investor in that mortgage does not lose money if they have paid for a credit default swap. Instead, they are granted the unpaid fees by the mortgage's lender. In this case, that lender was AIG.

When AIG started selling credit default swaps, it had no idea that so many subprime mortgages would go bad. Because credit default swaps were sold at a higher price than other securities, AIG figured that selling the swaps would provide it with a good deal of extra income. When borrowers started defaulting on their loans, however, AIG was forced to give its investors the amount unpaid by the borrowers of its subprime mortgages. This cost was too great for AIG to handle. It had no choice but to seek a bailout.

This would be the second bailout AIG had requested from the federal government. Previously, it had received billions of dollars in government funds to help with its liquidity crisis, a situation caused by its inability to receive bank loans due to a decrease in its credit rating. Unfortunately, AIG's trouble with subprime mortgages

Bailout funds given to AIG would help repay investors who had lost money by investing in subprime mortgages.

further reduced its credit rating. This crisis forced the corporation to pay more than $10 billion to its various creditors, a cost that pushed it into bankruptcy. AIG's second bailout gave it access to $85 billion in federal funds. In exchange, the federal government would receive rights to nearly 80 percent of AIG's preferred stock, in addition to loan fees.

Additional victims of the subprime mortgage crisis included financial services firms Citigroup and Bank of America. Like Bear Stearns and Lehman Brothers, Citigroup was facing the consequences that came with subprime mortgage lending. It was forced to lay off tens of thousands of employees before receiving billions of dollars from the federal government. Bank of America, meanwhile, had suffered losses after acquiring Merrill Lynch, a financial firm riddled with debt due to dealing in subprime mortgages. Bank of America was bailed out by the government in early 2009.

The subprime mortgage crisis was just the beginning of the early 2000s recession. The bankruptcy of big investment firms had caused a slowdown of the entire economy. All types of businesses, from restaurants to bookstores, were facing financial hardship. Few other areas of business, however, would be hit as hard as the auto industry.

The Automotive Crisis

Secretary Timothy F. Geithner
Department of the Treasury

Neil Barofsky
Special Inspector General SIGTARP

Another contributor to the recession of the early 2000s was a major increase in gas prices. This increase was due to the depletion of the world's petroleum resources, which leads to higher prices from oil companies. Higher gas prices meant bad news for America's biggest automotive companies: Chrysler, General Motors, and Ford. Known as the "Big Three," these companies mainly focused on making sport utility vehicles and trucks—vehicles that require a great deal of gas to run. With gas prices at around $4 per gallon in 2008, many Americans weren't willing to purchase these gas-guzzling vehicles. More people were leaning toward fuel-efficient vehicles, which require less gas and are better for the environment. At the time, these vehicles were being made by the Big Three's competitors.

Many people criticized the Big Three for not designing fuel-efficient vehicles themselves during a time when petroleum was becoming a rare resource. Many

Many car dealerships were forced to close when the Big Three began to lose business; some held sales at which cars were priced much lower than their original market values.

felt that the Big Three were also damaging the environment, since SUVs emit more dangerous greenhouse gases than other vehicles.

Investors took notice as more people turned their backs on the Big Three. They knew business for Chrysler, GM, and Ford was in trouble and that they should therefore invest their money elsewhere. Even people who were still fans of trucks and SUVs couldn't provide enough business to keep the Big Three profitable. The subprime mortgage crisis had made it such that few people had the money to purchase new vehicles. New vehicle sales were at their lowest level in twenty-five years.

Another factor in the Big Three's failure was labor union negotiations. Labor unions are organizations of workers that bargain with their employers for better working conditions. The Big Three's employees belonged to the United Auto Workers (UAW), which had established strict rules about how much its members would be paid. It was reported in 2008 that UAW workers made $74 per hour, while Toyota employees made $44 per hour. Critics complained that the Big Three shouldn't have allowed the UAW to talk them into paying such high salaries.

The Big Three Bailout

As business continued to decline, the Big Three asked the government for assistance. In late 2008, the CEOs of the Big Three—Rick Wagoner of GM, Alan Mulally of Ford, and Robert Nardelli of Chrysler—went together to Washington, D.C., to request $25 billion in bailout funds. Their request would be heard at a bailout hearing, a formal meeting during which Congress interviews corporate executives in order to decide whether or not they should be granted a bailout.

Unfortunately, the bailout hearing for the three automakers did not go very well. Government officials were appalled to learn that the automotive executives

The Big Three executives came under public scrutiny when their hearing was aired on television. Many thought it was shameful for the executives to ask for bailout funds after flying to Washington in expensive jets.

attending the hearing had flown to Washington on private jets. Congress felt that if the automakers were really in need of funds, they wouldn't be spending so much money on interstate travel.

"It's almost like seeing a guy show up at the soup kitchen in a high hat and tuxedo," scolded Representative Gary Ackerman of New York during the bailout hearing. "Couldn't you all have downgraded to first class or jet-pooled or something to get here? It would have at least sent a message that you do get it."

The hearing, which was televised, became the talk of the nation. The public was outraged by the idea that their tax dollars could be spent on business executives wealthy enough to fly in private jets. "What do they need money for?" many wanted to know. The government insisted, however, that private jets or not, the Big Three were definitely in financial trouble. Allowing the Big Three to go bankrupt, the government decided, would be devastating to the economy. In December 2008, President George W. Bush approved a $17.4 billion bailout of the corporations provided that the companies limit their executives' salaries and stop using private jets.

The Troubled Asset Relief Program

The $17.4 billion automotive industry bailout was funded by the Troubled Asset Relief Program, otherwise known as TARP. A $700 billion fund, TARP was created to assist corporations facing bankruptcy during the recession. TARP dollars, which are provided by taxpayers, are given to companies in exchange for troubled assets, which are securities of little value, such as subprime mortgages. TARP is run by the Office of Financial Stability, which was created by the Emergency Economic Stabilization Act of 2008. In order to qualify for TARP funds, corporations must be established, regulated financial institutions with significant operations in the United States. In other words, they must be large, powerful corporations with many American customers. Corporations receiving TARP funds are also asked to

President Obama's auto task force was formed to deal with the bailout of Chrysler and General Motors. The group reviewed the companies' restructuring plans and made recommendations that would help keep companies from going out of business.

give up certain tax benefits and limit the salaries of their executives.

A Second Bailout?

After receiving shares of the $17.4 billion bailout, Chrysler and GM executives asked the government for more. They believed that they would need an additional $22 billion if they were to become competitive corporations again. The public majority was very much against a second bailout of the automotive industry. Many were still upset by the private jet incident. Some people were simply more interested in seeing the money channeled to more worthy causes.

It was up to newly elected President Barack Obama to lead the government in its decision of whether or not to give Chrysler and GM the money that they were seeking. President Obama knew this would be a difficult task. On one hand, he did not want to upset people who were opposed to the second bailout. On the other hand, he did not want to watch thousands of automotive employees lose their jobs. The choice was one that he would have to take seriously.

President Obama assembled a special auto task force to help him make his decision. He told the Chrysler and GM executives that in order to receive their $22 billion, they would have to come up with separate plans for cutting costs and becoming more trustworthy, responsible corporations. He and his task force would decide, following a series of meetings with the two corporations, if the plans they presented were acceptable.

In March 2009, President Obama announced that it was his and his task force's opinion that Chrysler and GM had not created strong enough plans for restructuring their companies. However, he also acknowledged that the struggling automotive industry, which had lost more than four hundred thousand jobs in the past year, could not afford to fail. While he would not approve of giving the companies the $22 billion that they had asked for, he promised that he would do his best to prevent them from going out of business.

The president made a public announcement that the government would assist the failing automotive companies, but only if the companies made solid efforts to improve their business practices.

After reviewing GM's plan, the president decided that this corporation had at least tried to change its business for the better. He therefore reported that the government would give the company enough money to operate for sixty days while he and his administration helped it to come up with a better course of action. He was not so generous with Chrysler, however. The president was completely unimpressed with the plan the company had presented and was unsure that he could trust the company to continue to operate on its own. He did promise it $6 billion, but only if Chrysler merged with Italian automaker Fiat within the next thirty days.

The Chrysler-Fiat Future

Chrysler employees worked to remain positive as the company proceeded with its merger with Fiat. By partnering with the Italian automaker, Chrysler hoped to satisfy both the government and the public by relying less on the manufacturing of trucks and SUVs. Chrysler was also hoping to become more of an upscale brand of car. In a quote from *Automotive News*, current Chrysler-Fiat CEO Peter Fong describes the new Chrysler vehicle as being "a notch above Lincoln, a notch above Cadillac." Unfortunately, many of the new products it has introduced to the market since claiming bankruptcy have been SUVs. Fiat now owns 20 percent of Chrysler, without having to invest any cash into the struggling company.

Much of America disagreed with the way President Obama handled the Big Three's bailout. People were concerned that the president was exercising too much power over private companies. Of course, corporate bailouts have always been the subject of controversy. There are many reasons why people are either for or against this method of assisting the economy.

Corporate Bailout Controversy

Corporate bailouts continue to be a controversial topic today. The issue is especially subject to debate within the United States. This is partly because many Americans believe it is unconstitutional for the government to interfere in private business practices.

As a democratic nation, no one person, group, or institution within the United States is allowed to have supreme power. Checks and balances—a series of rules included in the U.S. Constitution—ensure that no government branch becomes too powerful. If the cabinet, Senate, or any other government entity makes a decision entirely on its own, it is disregarding the Constitution and its system of checks and balances.

How Do Checks and Balances Work?

Power is distributed evenly among the three main branches of the U.S. government: the executive, legislative, and judicial branches. Potential laws, or bills, are

Members of the legislative branch usually vote by saying "aye" or "nay," with the presiding officer announcing the results of the vote according to which group voiced their opinion the loudest.

introduced by the legislative branch, which is made up of the Senate and House of Representatives.

If the legislative branch votes in favor of a bill, the bill is then reviewed by the executive branch, which includes the president, vice president, and the cabinet—a group of presidential advisers. If the president does not agree with the bill, he or she has the power to veto, or vote against it. However, a vetoed bill does not simply die. Instead, it returns to the legislative branch and gets voted on again. With enough votes, the legislative branch can reverse the president's veto and turn the bill into law. Checks and balances don't stop there, however. Should a member of the public disagree agree with the new law, he or she can file a lawsuit and ask the judicial branch to review the law and decide whether or not it is truly constitutional.

Checks and Balances During a Recession

Throughout the history of corporate bailouts, certain branches of the government have demanded things from corporations without first abiding by the system of checks and balances. For example, during the automotive crisis, President Obama and his auto task force ordered Chrysler to merge with Fiat without first properly checking with the legislative branch. Many Americans felt this type of executive decision was unconstitutional, and that the president was wielding too much power over the automotive industry.

There are government officials, as well as members of the general public, who insist that there is no time to ensure accurate checks and balances when the country is in a recession. Bills can take years to turn into law, and if the unemployment rate is rising each day, it's only natural for people to demand that the government provide a solution as soon as possible. These people may say that in times of crisis, it is sometimes necessary for

American citizens against the bailouts wave flags and hold signs during the bailout protest in an attempt to express their opinion.

the government to take a stronger leadership role. Their opponents tend to warn them, however, that overlooking the Constitution means overlooking the most important ideals that America was founded on.

Another antibailout argument is that bailouts actually weaken the economy by burdening people with taxes. Some people point out that with more taxes to pay, they'll be even less likely to spend money on the goods, services, and securities belonging to businesses receiving bailouts. People also dislike the idea of having

The world is watching and waiting for President Obama to come up with a way to help end the recession. Many people wonder how far he will continue to go in supporting corporate bailouts.

to spend tax dollars on bailing out a corporation that may have been frivolous or unwise with its money.

The government's response to the claim that bailouts are bad for the economy because they mean an increase in taxes has usually been this: Sometimes things have to get worse before they get better. In other words, people may have to pay more taxes now, but doing so means they will not have to suffer as much in the future. People who agree with this statement may also urge others to understand that by spending tax dol-

lars on bailouts, they are not just paying for corporations' well-being. They are paying for the well-being of
the economy as a whole. The recession has proven that
should a big enough corporation go bankrupt, it can
mean trouble for all of America.

Not all government officials are in agreement with
corporate bailouts. Conservative representatives, who
usually favor the free market, are widely against TARP,
the $700 billion pool of government funds reserved for
failing corporations. The free market is the idea that
businesses should rise and fall on their own, without
government intervention.

It's not only conservative politicians who disagree
with corporate bailouts. A number of liberals in the leg-
islature also continue to point out that bailouts are too
big a burden for taxpayers. TARP is also said to be toxic
for taxpayers: Of the $573 billion that taxpayers have
put into the fund, only $72.8 billion has been returned.
Forty companies that received TARP funds have repaid
the public, but that leaves 655 who have yet to do so.
Experts say that taxpayers could end up putting $23.7
trillion into TARP if other bailout programs fail.

Both parties are working on methods for at least pre-
venting future bailouts. President Obama and his
administration recently introduced a proposal for a consumer financial protection agency. The agency would set
new standards for ordinary mortgages, prevent risky

loans, and protect credit card customers. Those in favor of the agency say that consumer regulation must be established in order to stop the type of bad business practices that caused the subprime mortgage crisis. Opponents to the agency include mortgage brokers and investment firms that dislike the idea of being further controlled by the government.

Meanwhile, many government conservatives are lobbying for the creation of an independent trust to deal with shaky corporations. A trust is an institution that manages finances on behalf of another party. Many conservatives feel that it is better for businesses to report to an independent trust than to the government.

With the country still reeling from the recession of the early 2000s, it remains difficult to say if corporate bailouts will prove to be a successful method for saving the economy. Many continue to hope that the government will find a more constitutional way to ensure financial recovery. Until then, the debate will continue, although there is one thing that all parties agree on: It is important for corporations and the government to be more responsible in the future in order to ensure that we don't endure another economic crisis.

Glossary

asset An item of ownership convertible into cash.

bankrupt At the end of one's resources.

broker An agent who buys or sells without having title to the property.

credit To supply goods or services without immediate payment.

default Failure to meet financial obligations.

economy The prosperity or earnings of a place.

exempt Free from an obligation.

finance To supply with money.

hijack To seize a vehicle by force or threat of force.

income The monetary payment received for goods and services.

interest A sum paid or charged for borrowing money.

interstate Connecting or involving different states.

investor A person or agency that invests money.

liability Money owed.

loan To lend money at interest.

recipient A person that receives.

securities Stocks or bonds.

taxes Money demanded by a government for specific services.

terrorist A person, usually a member of a group, who uses or threatens violence for political purposes.

For More Information

Consolidated Rail Corporation (Conrail)
1717 Arch Street
Philadelphia PA 19103
(215) 209-2000
Web site: http://www.conrail.com
Now owned by the CSX Corporation, Conrail provides freight service in parts of the northeast United States.

Fannie Mae
3900 Wisconsin Avenue NW
Washington, DC 20016-2892
(202) 752-7000
Web site: http://www.fanniemae.com
Fannie Mae is a government-sponsored enterprise created to stabilize the housing market.

Federal Housing Finance Agency (FHFA)
1700 G Street NW
4th Floor
Washington, DC 20552
(866) 796-5595
Web site: http://www.fhfa.gov
The FHFA regulates Fannie Mae, Freddie Mac, and twelve other housing banks.

Freddie Mac

8200 Jones Branch Drive

McLean, VA 22102-3110

(703) 903-2000

Web site: http://www.freddiemac.com

Freddie Mac is a government-sponsored enterprise created to stabilize the housing market. It is one of America's biggest buyers of home mortgages, started by Congress in 1970.

Royal Bank of Canada (RBC)

200 Bay Street, Royal Bank Plaza

Toronto, ON M5J 2J5

Canada

(800) 769-2511

Web site: http://www.rbcroyalbank.com

The RBC is Canada's biggest bank, as well as its biggest company.

Treasury Management Association of Canada (TMAC)

1010–8 King Street East

Toronto, ON M5C 1B5

Canada

(416) 367-8500

Web site: http://www.tmac.ca

The TMAC is Canada's only national association of treasury and financial professionals. It offers educational seminars on a variety of financial topics.

U.S. Department of the Treasury
1500 Pennsylvania Avenue NW
Washington, DC 20220
(202) 622-6415
Web site: http://www.ustreas.gov
The U.S. Department of the Treasury manages the government's finances and works to promote economic growth and stability.

Web Sites

Due to the changing nature of Internet links, Rosen Publishing has developed an online list of Web sites related to the subject of this book. This site is updated regularly. Please use this link to access the list:

http://www.rosenlinks.com/itn/bail

For Further Reading

Berg, Adriane G., Arthur Bochner, and Rose Bochner. *The New, Totally Awesome Business Book for Kids.* 3rd ed. New York, NY: Newmarket, 2007.

Challen, Paul. *How Do Mortgages, Loans, and Credit Work?* New York, NY: Crabtree Publishing Company, 2009.

Daniels, Kathryn, Ann M. Williams, and Jane A. Williams. *Common Sense Business for Kids.* Placerville, CA: Bluestocking Press, 2006.

Hamilton, Jill. *Bankruptcy.* Farmington Hills, MI: Greenhaven Press, 2010.

Liebowitz, Jay. *Wall Street Wizard: Sound Ideas from a Savvy Teen Investor.* New York, NY: Simon and Schuster, 2000.

McLeish, Ewan. *Energy Crisis.* New York, NY: Franklin Watts, 2008.

Orr, Tamra. *A Kid's Guide to Stock Market Investing.* Hockessin, DE: Mitchell Lane Publishers, 2008.

Scott, David L. *Wall Street Words: An A to Z Guide to Investment Terms for Today's Investor.* Boston, MA: Houghton Mifflin, 2003.

Taylor-Butler, Christine. *The Congress of the United States.* Danbury, CT: Children's Press, 2008.

Bibliography

Anderson, Kurt. *Reset: How This Crisis Can Restore Our Values and Renew America.* New York, NY: Random House, 2009.

Ciferri, Luca. "Chrysler-Fiat's Grand Brand Plan." *Automotive News*, September 21, 2009. Retrieved December 10, 2009 (http://www.autonews.com/article/20090921/ANA03/309219951).

CNN Money. "The Fortune 500's Biggest Winners." CNNMoney.com, April 20, 2009. Retrieved December 10, 2009 (http://money.cnn.com/galleries/2009/fortune/0904/gallery.f500_mostprofitable.fortune/index.html).

Cooper Ramo, Joshua. *The Age of the Unthinkable: Why the New World Disorder Constantly Surprises the U.S. and What We Can Do About It.* New York, NY: Little, Brown and Company, 2009.

Federal Deposit Insurance Corporation. "FDIC Law, Regulations, Related Acts." July 30, 2009. Retrieved December 10, 2009 (http://www.fdic.gov/regulations/laws/rules/8000-3100.html).

Feldman, Ron J., and Gary H. Stern. *Too Big to Fail: The Hazards of Bank Bailouts.* Washington, DC: 2004.

Gay Stolberg, Sheryl, and Bill Vlasic. "U.S. Lays Down Terms for Auto Bailout." *New York Times*, March 30,

2009. Retrieved December 10, 2009 (http://www. nytimes.com/2009/03/30/business/30auto.html? pagewanted=1&_r=1).

Huffington Post. "TARP Anniversary: By the Numbers." HuffingtonPost.com, October 2, 2009. Retrieved December 10, 2009 (http://www.huffingtonpost.com/ 2009/10/02/tarp-anniversary-by-the-n_n_307643.html).

Jickling, Mark. "CRS Report for Congress: Fannie Mae and Freddie Mac in Conservatorship." September 15, 2008. Retrieved December 10, 2009 (http://fpc.state. gov/documents/organization/110097.pdf).

Lewis, Josh. "Big Three Auto CEOs Flew Private Jets to Ask for Taxpayer Money." CNN.com, November 19, 2008. Retrieved December 10, 2009 (http://www.cnn. com/2008/US/11/19/autos.ceo.jets/index.html).

Phillips, Kevin. *Bad Money: Reckless Finance, Failed Politics, and the Global Crisis of American Capitalism.* New York, NY: Penguin Books, 2008.

United Press International. "Henry Paulson Quotes." UPI.com. Retrieved December 10, 2009 (http://www. upi.com/topic/Henry_Paulson/quotes).

Index

About the Author

Bethany Bezdecheck lives with her husband and dog in Hoboken, New Jersey. She has written on a variety of nonfiction topics for children and young adults.

Photo Credits

Cover (top left), p. 5 Joe Raedle/Getty Images; cover (top right) Stan Honda/AFP/Getty Images; cover (bottom) Emmanuel Dunand/AFP/Getty Images; pp. 4, 9 Justin Sullivan/Getty Images; pp. 7, 52 UPI/Newscom; p. 12 Scott J. Ferrell/Congressional Quarterly/Getty Images; pp. 14, 18 Fox Photos/Hulton Archive/Getty Images; pp. 15, 20, 22 © AP Images; p. 25 Tim Boyle/Getty Images; pp. 27, 31 Chris Hondros/Getty Images; pp. 28, 40 Scott Olson/Getty Images; p. 33 AFP/Newscom; p. 37 Newscom; pp. 39, 44 Win McNamee/Getty Images; p. 42 Brendan Hoffman/Getty Images; p. 46 Alex Wong/Getty Images; pp. 48, 51 David McNew/Getty Images; p. 49 Chip Somodevilla/Getty Images.

Designer: Tom Forget; Editor: Bethany Bryan;
Photo Researcher: Cindy Reiman